WITHDRAWN
FROM THE RECORDS OF THE
MID-CONTINENT PUBLIC LIBRARY

AMAZING EXPEDITIONS

JOURNEYS THAT CHANGED THE WORLD

· ANITA GANERI ·

ILLUSTRATED BY

MICHAEL MULLAN

IVY KIDS

· CONTENTS ·

· INTRODUCTION ·

Throughout history, explorers have bravely ventured out into the unknown to discover new lands, seek treasure, make scientific discoveries, or simply achieve something that's never been done before. This book will take you on a voyage over oceans, deserts, and mountains, through jungles, ice, and cities, and even launch you into space! You'll discover 22 extraordinary explorers and learn how their amazing expeditions changed our world.

Some of these journeys ended in failure or tragedy—but that doesn't mean they're not interesting or valuable. Mistakes can lead to great discoveries, and most explorers are remembered for their perseverance and grit, as much as for their successes.

Exploration has revealed many mysteries of the world, but in some cases it also had terrible consequences, especially for the people already living in the lands being explored. It's important to look back and remember the good and the bad so that future explorers can learn from the past.

Every expedition has its own particular purpose behind it, which is sometimes connected to the time in history that it took place.

· 1 ·
Early exploration

Some of the first explorations we know about took place around the Mediterranean Sea during the 5th and 4th centuries BCE. Hanno the Navigator's voyage is a prime example. His mission was to find new lands for his people to settle in and, on the way, he encountered extraordinary things like volcanoes, crocodiles, and gorillas!

· 2 ·
Age of Discovery

Between the 15th and 17th centuries, European explorers undertook long and daring sea voyages to find new trade routes and partners to exchange goods with. Some of the most famous explorers in history were voyaging in this time, including Christopher Columbus, Vasco da Gama, and Ferdinand Magellan. Between them, they colonized (invaded and settled in) vast parts of the Americas, Africa, Asia, and Australia and Oceania, changing the world forever.

· 3 ·
In the name of science

Beginning in the 18th century, there was a change in exploration that continues to this day. Scientific discovery was the new motivator, and explorers were keen to improve the world's knowledge of Earth, even if it meant risking their lives. One such explorer was Mary Kingsley, who defied stereotypes and plunged into African jungles, facing wild animals and even living with cannibals—all in the name of science. Or Neil Armstrong, who explored farther than ever before... all the way to the Moon!

· 4 ·
Modern explorers

Today, in the 21st century, most of our Earth has been explored. Far-flung places, such as Antarctica, can now be visited by tourists—there are even plans to fly tourists into space! Today's explorers are largely scientists and conservationists, trying to develop knowledge of our fragile planet and the many threats it faces.

More reasons to explore

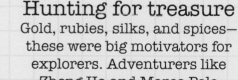

Hunting for treasure
Gold, rubies, silks, and spices—these were big motivators for explorers. Adventurers like Zheng He and Marco Polo traveled the world in search of treasures to bring home for their countries and themselves!

Adventure
Glory and personal achievement have inspired some of the most famous expeditions of all time. These adventures have a habit of being either spectacular successes or deadly disasters! Either way, they have become legendary—from Amelia Earhart's fateful flight to Tenzing Norgay and Edmund Hillary's Everest success.

Religious calling
Exploration isn't always driven by nations searching to conquer new lands. Some expeditions have a more personal and often religious purpose. Xuanzang, Ibn Battuta, and David Livingstone are all explorers who set out on solitary religious journeys.

· A KEY TO THE MAPS ·

Nearly all of the journeys in this book feature maps
to help you visualize the expeditions.

Maps are important tools. They tell us all kinds of
things, from where rivers start and the size of
continents, to which countries are neighbors.

Humans haven't always had a complete map of Earth.
For a long while, our understanding of the world was like
a gigantic jigsaw puzzle, with lots of pieces missing and
some pieces squished into the wrong spaces!

Explorers like Christopher Columbus, Meriwether Lewis,
and William Clark changed this with their amazing
expeditions and helped us piece the jigsaw together.

Without maps, Ellen MacArthur would have
struggled to win her record-breaking race,
and with better maps, perhaps James Cook
would have finally found Antarctica!

On the opposite page is a simple guide to help you
find your way around the maps in this book.

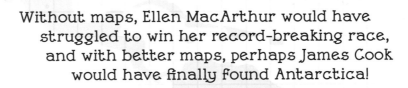

MAP SYMBOLS

———————— Red lines show the journey.

———————— Green lines show the return journey (if there is one).

——————▶ These arrows on the journey lines indicate the direction of the journey.

● Blue dots indicate countries.

● Red dots indicate cities or other places.

▲▲ Triangle shapes indicate mountains.

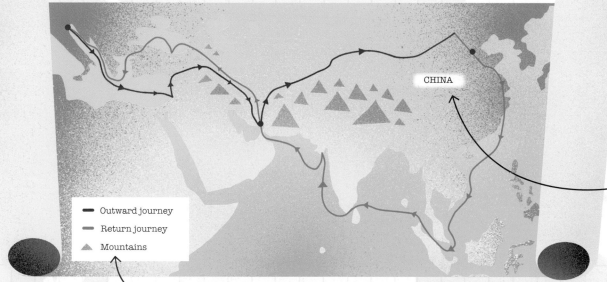

CHINA

All the maps have various labels, such as continent names, country names, place names, rivers, oceans, and other topographic features like deserts and glaciers. All the maps use modern-day place names.

— Outward journey
— Return journey
▲ Mountains

Most of the maps have little keys like this one to help you read them.

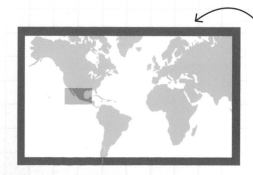

Some pages feature smaller maps like these. These maps are there to help you see in what part of the world the journey took place.

North Pole

South Pole

Hanno the Navigator

Born: 6th century BCE. Died: 5th century BCE.
Duration of exploration: Unknown

In the early 5th century BCE, an explorer called Hanno led a fleet of ships from the great trading city of Carthage, in modern-day Tunisia. Although his exact route is unknown, this was the first recorded voyage along the west coast of Africa. Along the way he faced hostile people, fierce gorillas, and erupting volcanoes.

· 1 ·

Hanno sailed from Carthage harbor with a fleet of 60 ships. His mission was to explore the west coast of Africa and set up colonies (settlements under the control of Carthage). On board the ships were food, supplies, and about 30,000 people who would stay at the colonies and build communities there.

PORTUGAL
SPAIN
ATLANTIC OCEAN
Strait of Gibraltar
Mediterranean Sea
AFRICA

· 2 ·

Early on in the voyage the fleet sailed through the Pillars of Hercules (the modern-day Strait of Gibraltar), a narrow passage linking the Mediterranean Sea to the Atlantic Ocean. The crew had no compass and relied on the stars for navigation.

· 3 ·

The fleet traveled down the western coast of Africa, sailing close to land for safety. Hanno established colonies along the coast of modern-day Morocco, allowing groups of settlers to disembark from the ships every few days. At one point the fleet stopped and built a temple to Poseidon, the Greek God of the sea.

· 4 ·

Continuing south, Hanno sailed up a great river, which some believe was the Senegal River. Here, he encountered elephants, hippos, and crocodiles—animals that he had never seen before.

· 5 ·

Some weeks later, the fleet sailed past a country that seemed to be on fire, with rivers of flames flowing into the sea. Hanno sensed the danger and quickly captained his fleet away to safety. Some historians say this was Mount Cameroon, a volcano that is still active today.

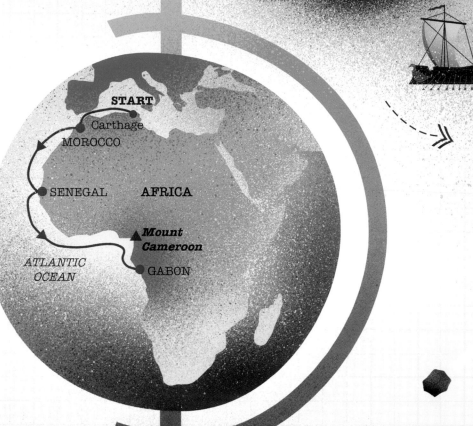

START
Carthage
MOROCCO

SENEGAL   AFRICA

▲ *Mount Cameroon*

ATLANTIC OCEAN   GABON

THE POSSIBLE ROUTE OF HANNO THE NAVIGATOR

· 6 ·

Hanno next reached an island where he encountered wild, hairy creatures. He thought they were humans, but they may have been gorillas! They were ferocious and threw stones at Hanno's people.

· 7 ·

Shortly afterward, with food and water running low, Hanno decided to head home. There are no details of the return journey, and we don't know exactly how far south he had traveled. But some believe he made it all the way to modern-day Gabon.

· 8 ·

Back home in Carthage, Hanno regaled his people with the story of his journey and his epic adventures were carved on a stone tablet. But the tablet was lost when the city was destroyed by the Romans in 146 BCE. Luckily, a Greek translation survived, though some parts were still missing.

HANNO'S LEGACY

No one knows what happened to Hanno after his expedition and historians continue to argue about the facts of his journey. But his voyage has become legendary and today he is classified as one of history's greatest explorers.

Xuanzang

Born: c. 602 Died: c. 664
Duration of exploration: c. 629–645

Xuanzang was born in China and became a Buddhist monk at just 13 years old. Buddhists follow the teachings of Siddhartha Gautama, the Buddha, who went on a quest for Enlightenment in the 6th century BCE. Enlightenment is a spiritual state and is all about understanding the nature of life. Xuanzang spent years in a monastery studying his religion, but he wanted to know more. Legend says that he had a dream, encouraging him to make the long and risky overland journey to India, where Buddhism began.

· 2 ·

Xuanzang headed north across the Gobi Desert with his horse. The journey was grueling and dangerous. Xuanzang nearly died of thirst when he dropped his water canteen. But he survived and continued his journey.

· 1 ·

In 629, the part of China that Xuanzang lived in was at war and foreign travel was banned. But Xuanzang was determined to reach India and enrich his knowledge of Buddhism. He left in secret, traveling by night and resting by day.

· 3 ·

When he reached the city of Turpan in northwest China, his luck improved. The King of Turpan was also a Buddhist and admired Xuanzang. He gave him money, horses, and letters of introduction to help him on his travels.

· 4 ·

Next, Xuanzang followed the Silk Road (an ancient network of trade routes that connected the East and West). He faced deserts, mountains, robbers, and heavy snow, but eventually he reached Samarkand in modern-day Uzbekistan. The city was a great trading center bustling with merchants and goods.

· 5 ·

As he continued on his journey, Xuanzang marveled at the sights he saw. While passing through Afghanistan, he struggled through the Hindu Kush mountains to reach the Buddhas of Bamiyan, two gigantic statues that had been carved into the rock face.

· 6 ·

In 630, Xuanzang reached India. He spent years traveling, visiting sacred sites, following the path of the Buddha, and meeting fellow monks. He spent two years at Nalanda monastery, one of India's first universities. Studying here, Xuanzang felt he had achieved his journey's purpose.

· 7 ·

In 643, Xuanzang began his long journey home. He had collected more than 600 Buddhist texts, statues, and other artifacts. But disaster struck as he was crossing the Indus River by boat and 50 of the precious manuscripts were lost overboard in a storm.

· 8 ·

Xuanzang reached China in 645, having spent 16 years away from home. He was given a hero's welcome by the emperor and offered many honors and rewards, which he refused. Instead, he retired to a monastery where he spent the remaining 19 years of his life, translating his Indian texts into Chinese.

UZBEKISTAN

Samarkand

Turpan

Gobi Desert

START
Chang'an
(Xi'an)

CHINA

AFGHANISTAN

Nalanda

INDIA

Arabian Sea

Bay of Bengal

— Outward journey

— Return journey

Xuanzang's Travels

11

Marco Polo

Born: 1254 Died: 1324
Duration of exploration: 1271–1295

Marco Polo was born in Venice, Italy, into a wealthy family. His father and uncle traveled widely across Europe to Asia, buying and selling jewels. In 1271, aged just 17, Marco joined them on a great adventure to the court of Kublai Khan—the mighty emperor of Mongolia and China.

· 1 ·

In 1271, Marco Polo, his father, Niccolò, and uncle, Maffeo, set off from Venice and sailed to Jerusalem. They were on a mission from Kublai Khan. Niccolò and Maffeo had met him a few years before and he had asked them to bring him oil from a special lamp in Jerusalem. The lamp was believed to burn eternally and its oil was said to be holy.

· 5 ·

Finally, in 1275, four years after their departure, the Polos reached the city of Shangdu in China and the palace of Kublai Khan. They gave him the oil and other gifts and messages. The Khan was impressed by Marco and offered him a job.

· 4 ·

Next, they joined a camel train of travelers to cross the deadly Gobi Desert. The desert was said to be haunted and filled with ghostly, drumming sounds. One day, during a sandstorm, they were attacked by bandits. The Polos escaped but many of their fellow travelers were killed.

· 2 ·

They collected the oil and traveled by camel to the port of Hormuz (in modern-day Iran). They planned to sail the rest of the way to China, but their ships were in poor condition. So they continued overland following the Silk Road (an ancient network of trade routes that connected the East and West).

· 3 ·

The journey was exhausting. They faced storms and illness, and at one point they had to climb the treacherous, ice-covered slopes of the Pamir Mountains. These are some of the world's highest peaks, on the borders of modern-day Pakistan, China, and India.

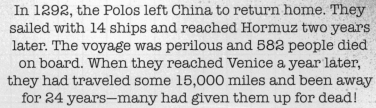

· 6 ·

For the next 17 years, Marco traveled widely around China and Asia on official business for the Khan. He saw many wonderful sights and places, including the island of Sri Lanka, famous for its dazzling rubies and gemstones.

· 7 ·

In 1292, the Polos left China to return home. They sailed with 14 ships and reached Hormuz two years later. The voyage was perilous and 582 people died on board. When they reached Venice a year later, they had traveled some 15,000 miles and been away for 24 years—many had given them up for dead!

· 8 ·

The adventure wasn't over. Venice was at war with the Republic of Genoa, and Marco joined the fight. He was captured and thrown into prison. After three years he was released. The treasures he had collected on his travels made him a wealthy man. He settled into life in Venice, married, and had three children.

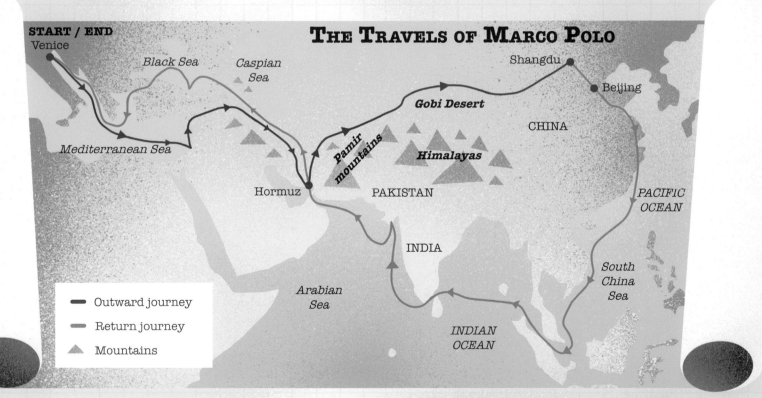

THE TRAVELS OF MARCO POLO

START / END
Venice

Black Sea

Caspian Sea

Shangdu

Beijing

Mediterranean Sea

Gobi Desert

CHINA

Pamir mountains

Himalayas

Hormuz

PAKISTAN

PACIFIC OCEAN

Arabian Sea

INDIA

South China Sea

INDIAN OCEAN

— Outward journey
— Return journey
▲ Mountains

MARCO POLO'S LEGACY

In prison, Marco shared his cell with a writer called Rustichello. Marco told Rustichello about his travels and Rustichello wrote them down in a book. They called it *The Book of the Marvels of the World*. It was a bestseller and inspired future explorers.

Ibn Battuta

Born: 1304 Died: 1368
Duration of exploration: 1325–1354

Ibn Battuta was born in Morocco and was a devout Muslim. As a young man, he studied Islamic law and decided to make a pilgrimage (a religious journey), called the hajj, to the city of Mecca (a sacred place for Muslims where Muhammad, the Prophet, was born) in Saudi Arabia. This started an incredible 29-year journey, covering 74,500 miles.

· 1 ·

Aged 21, Ibn Battuta set off alone on his first hajj to Mecca. He was sad to leave his family but determined to go. He would not return to Morocco for 24 years!

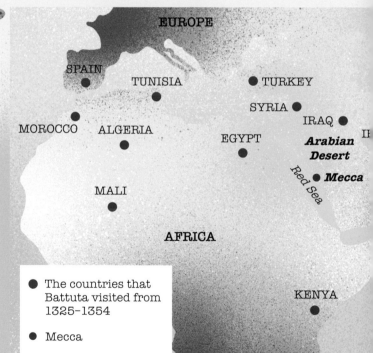

EUROPE

SPAIN
TUNISIA
TURKEY
SYRIA
IRAQ
MOROCCO
ALGERIA
EGYPT
Arabian Desert
Red Sea
Mecca
MALI
AFRICA
KENYA

● The countries that Battuta visited from 1325–1354

● Mecca

· 2 ·

He traveled through Tunisia and Algeria and faced illness, exhaustion, and loneliness. At one point, he joined a camel train which gave him company and safety. Then he visited Egypt and Syria, where he joined a group also heading to Mecca.

· 3 ·

In 1327, after crossing the desert in Syria, Battuta reached Mecca and completed his pilgrimage. Instead of returning home, however, he decided to continue his travels.

· 4 ·

He journeyed to Iraq, over the Zagros Mountains to Iran, and back again to Iraq. From there, Battuta crossed the Arabian Desert and returned to Mecca in 1328, completing a second hajj. But he still wasn't ready to return to Morocco, and this time, he planned a sea voyage.

· 6 ·

In around 1331, Battuta traveled to India. His route took him through Russia and Turkey. From there, he journeyed to Afghanistan and trekked through the deadly Hindu Kush mountains, reaching India in 1333. Battuta spent nine years there, working as a judge for the mighty Sultan of Delhi.

· 5 ·

Sailing along the Red Sea coast, Battuta visited many Muslim kingdoms in East Africa, reaching as far south as Mombasa in modern-day Kenya. Then, once again, he returned to Mecca for his third hajj in 1330. But still his desire to travel kept him from home.

· 7 ·

In 1342, the sultan sent Battuta to China as his ambassador. The journey was a disaster. Battuta's ship sank before he even set off, and on the way he was nearly killed by pirates! He finally reached China in 1344.

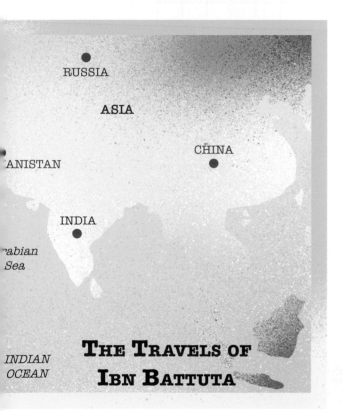

RUSSIA

ASIA

CHINA

ANISTAN

INDIA

abian
Sea

**THE TRAVELS OF
IBN BATTUTA**

INDIAN
OCEAN

· 8 ·

From China, Battuta headed for home at last, stopping at Mecca for a final hajj. He reached Morocco in 1349. He was now a wealthy and famous man. But for all his riches, Battuta did not have everything; sadly, both his parents had died before his return.

· 9 ·

Restless, Battuta could not settle. After a trip to Spain in 1351, where he avoided an outbreak of the plague, he made one last journey. He traveled across the scorching Sahara Desert to the city of Timbuktu in Mali, West Africa. There, he canoed down the Niger River and saw a hippopotamus for the first time!

· 10 ·

Battuta returned home for good in 1354. At the Sultan of Morocco's suggestion, he told his story to a court scholar. This amazing tale was published in a book called *The Travels*. Historians argue about the accuracy of the story. But there is no doubt that Ibn Battuta was one of history's greatest explorers.

Zheng He

Born: 1371 Died: 1433
Duration of exploration: 1405–1433

Zheng He was 10 years old when he was taken prisoner in China and forced to be a soldier. He worked his way up and went on to lead a huge fleet of ships, and about 28,000 men, on a series of daring voyages across the Indian Ocean. Their mission was to show the world how powerful China was, and to find safe routes at sea that would allow them to trade goods with other countries. The journeys came to be known as the "Treasure Voyages."

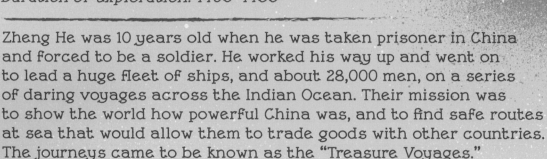

· 1 ·

In July 1405, Zheng He and his men prepared to set sail from the city of Nanjing on their first voyage. They prayed to Tianfei, the Chinese goddess of sailors, asking for her protection. Then Zheng He led his mighty fleet out across the seas.

· 2 ·

The fleet was made up of about 300 vessels, with enormous ships carrying gold, porcelain, and silk, as well as smaller ships carrying horses and soldiers. The ships were the biggest the world had ever seen! The crews communicated from ship to ship using flags in the day and colored lanterns at night.

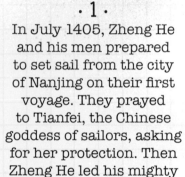

· 3 ·

During the voyage, Zheng He and his men sailed to Java in Indonesia and Sri Lanka before arriving at Calicut (modern-day Kozhikode) on the west coast of India. They traded their treasures for jewels and spices, such as cinnamon and ginger.

· 4 ·

The fleet was on its journey home when Zheng He and his men encountered Chen Zuyi, the most feared pirate of the time! In a bitter battle, Chen was defeated and about 5,000 of his men were killed. Zheng He sailed on to China.

Zheng He and his fleet reached home in 1407. The first trip had been a triumph. They had formed ties with foreign lands and discovered which countries might pose risks in the future. Zheng He also brought envoys (special messengers) from many lands. These envoys offered gifts and gave their allegiance to the Emperor of China.

After the success of the first voyage, Zheng He and his men returned to the seas in early 1408. They went on five more successful Treasure Voyages, until the emperor died in 1424 and the new ruler banned them. But Zheng He still took to the seas on a seventh, and final, voyage. The route is unknown and it is thought that he died during or soon after the voyage in 1433 and was buried at sea.

ZHENG HE'S TREASURE VOYAGES

— The route of Zheng He's first Treasure Voyage

● Some of the countries the fleet visited over the six journeys

Black Sea

Caspian Sea

SAUDI ARABIA

IRAN

OMAN

YEMEN

AFRICA

SOMALIA

KENYA

Arabian Sea

MALDIVES

INDIAN OCEAN

Calicut (Kozhikode)

SRI LANKA

INDIA

BANGLADESH

Bay of Bengal

THAILAND

VIETNAM

MALAYSIA

CHINA

START Nanjing

East China Sea

South China Sea

On his fifth and sixth voyages, Zheng He traveled as far as modern-day Kenya. On these voyages, envoys from Africa returned with the fleet to present the emperor with gifts, including gems and ivory, as well as zebras and giraffes.

ZHENG HE'S LEGACY

Today, Zheng He is recognized as a great explorer and a key figure in Chinese history. There has even been a TV series about him!

Christopher Columbus

Born: 1451 Died: 1506
Duration of exploration: 1492–1504

Christopher Columbus was born in Genoa (in modern-day Italy). In Columbus's time, European rulers wanted to trade with Asia for its valuable silks and spices, but the main routes were crowded and difficult to navigate. Columbus proposed a daring idea to reach Asia by sailing west across the Atlantic Ocean—a new and unknown route!

· 1 ·

Columbus needed ships, crew, supplies, and money, so he tried to persuade some European rulers to fund his voyage. But he was unsuccessful. They said his calculations were wrong, the Atlantic Ocean was too vast, and they thought he would fail.

NORTH AMERICA

ATLANTIC OCEAN

THE BAHAMAS

CUBA

HISPANIOLA

CENTRAL AMERICA

JAMAICA

TRINIDA

VENEZUELA

SOUTH AMERICA

The Voyages of Columbus

· 2 ·

Eventually, Columbus convinced Queen Isabella and King Ferdinand of Castille (in modern-day Spain) to back him. In August 1492, he set sail from Spain with three ships—the *Santa Maria*, the *Pinta*, and the *Nina*. He set his course west and headed into the unknown!

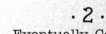

· 3 ·

Unfortunately, Columbus's calculations were indeed wrong and the fleet spent five long weeks on the open sea with no sight of land. On board, food and water were running low.

· 4 ·

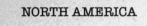

Finally, on October 11, a look-out spotted an island. Columbus thought they had reached Japan. In fact, they were in the Bahamas, thousands of miles away from Japan, in the Americas! Columbus claimed the island for Spain and named it San Salvador. Over the next weeks, he explored many more islands, including Cuba.

· 6 ·

In March 1493, Columbus was back in Spain, with gold and news of his success. He was welcomed like a hero by the king and queen.

· 5 ·

As Columbus explored, one of his ships was wrecked and had to be abandoned. He named the island they had landed on Hispaniola and left 40 settlers there. The fate of the people who already lived on these islands was terrible. Many were captured and killed, and most who survived were forced into slavery.

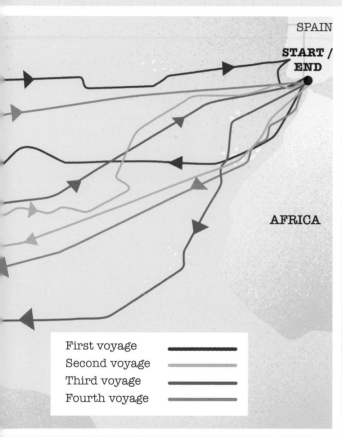

SPAIN

START / END

AFRICA

First voyage
Second voyage
Third voyage
Fourth voyage

· 7 ·

Later that year, Columbus returned to the Americas with 17 ships and more than 1,000 new settlers, who would remain in the "New World." The voyage was successful and Columbus discovered many more islands, including Guadeloupe and Saint Kitts, before returning to Spain.

· 8 ·

On a third voyage in 1498, Columbus explored farther than before, reaching Trinidad and the coast of modern-day Venezuela. Columbus realized he had reached a large landmass (South America), but he still believed he was in Asia!

· 9 ·

He returned to Hispaniola, but there was trouble ahead. The settlers were fed up—this "New World" did not meet their expectations and life was hard. Columbus was a harsh, violent ruler and he was hated for it. He was arrested and shipped back to Spain where he was imprisoned.

COLUMBUS'S LEGACY

Today Columbus divides opinion. He was an important historical figure, but his involvement in the terrible treatment of native peoples, the slave trade, and many other sad and shameful parts of history has not been forgotten.

· 10 ·

Despite this, Columbus was allowed to take one last voyage in 1502. He sailed along the coast of Central America before he was shipwrecked. He was stranded in Jamaica for a year before he was eventually rescued and returned to Spain. He died two years later, aged 55. Right to the end, he believed that he had reached Asia, and not the "New World" of the Americas!

Vasco da Gama

Born: 1460s Died: 1524
Duration of exploration: 1497–1499

In the 1490s, a young Portuguese soldier called Vasco da Gama set sail on a perilous voyage. His mission was to find a sea route to India so that Portugal could obtain rare, valuable spices. He decided to sail around Africa and cross the Indian Ocean. Many had tried and failed this route—now it was da Gama's turn. The journey would be full of danger but in the end, da Gama would achieve what no one else could.

· 1 ·
Da Gama set sail from Lisbon on July 8, 1497, with four ships and 170 men. He followed the route of another explorer, Bartolomeu Dias. Unlike Dias, who turned back at the Cape of Good Hope in Africa, da Gama was determined to make it to India.

· 2 ·
The fleet sailed south past the Cape Verde islands and into the South Atlantic Ocean. Instead of safely staying close to the coast, da Gama decided to sail out into the open sea, hoping for stronger winds. The winds were strong and the decision was right, but the fleet had to spend more than three months on the water with no sight of land.

· 3 ·
In December, they reached the tip of Africa, the point at which Dias had turned back. From now on, they were sailing into the unknown—no Europeans had ever sailed these seas. The terrified crew threatened to mutiny, so da Gama had the ringleaders put in chains.

· 4 ·
In March 1498, da Gama reached Mozambique, on the east coast of Africa, where he met with the sultan of Mozambique. Offended by the small gifts da Gama offered him, the Sultan forced the Portuguese fleet to leave. But da Gama had a vengeful, violent side and he fired his cannons into the city!

· 5 ·
The fleet sailed on to Malindi, in modern-day Kenya. Here, da Gama employed an Indian navigator with knowledge of monsoon winds (seasonal winds that bring heavy rains) to guide them across the Indian Ocean. With the guide's help, and the wind behind them, it took just 23 days for the ships to cross the ocean.

· 6 ·

In May 1498, da Gama reached Calicut (modern-day Kozhikode), and became the first European to sail around Africa and reach India by sea. Da Gama was welcomed by the King of Calicut but he didn't succeed in negotiating a trade deal for Portugal. Again, his gifts were not seen as good enough.

· 7 ·

An angry da Gama ignored the warnings of local sailors and set sail for home. But poor winds meant that it took 132 days to reach Malindi. The long months on the open waters had deadly consequences. Many of the crew fell ill with scurvy, caused by a lack of fresh fruit and vegetables. This made their hands and feet swell, and their gums so painful that they could not eat. By the time the fleet reached Lisbon, more than half of the crew had died.

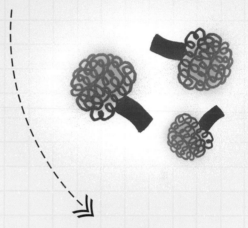

THE JOURNEY OF VASCO DA GAMA

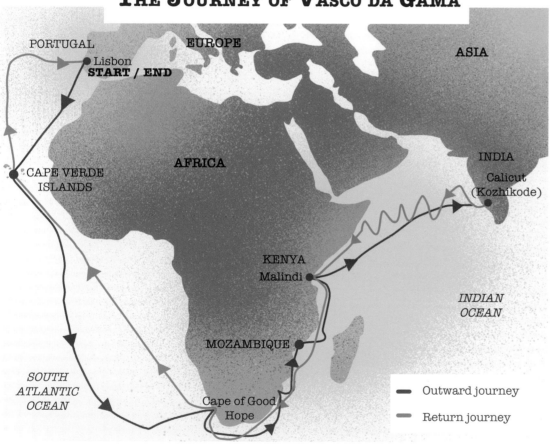

PORTUGAL
EUROPE
Lisbon
START / END
ASIA
AFRICA
CAPE VERDE
ISLANDS
INDIA
Calicut
(Kozhikode)
KENYA
Malindi
INDIAN
OCEAN
MOZAMBIQUE
SOUTH
ATLANTIC
OCEAN
Cape of Good
Hope

— Outward journey
— Return journey

· 8 ·

Back home, da Gama was treated like a hero. He had found a direct sea route to India and the spices he brought back were sold for huge profits. He settled into life, married, and had seven children, but the sea still tempted him.

· 9 ·

In 1502, war broke out between Calicut and Portugal. Da Gama sailed to India to force the king of Calicut to make peace. The king eventually signed a treaty and da Gama returned home, where he spent the next 20 years. In 1524, he voyaged to India again but caught malaria and died shortly after he arrived. His body was returned to Portugal and his tomb was decorated with gold and jewels.

Ferdinand Magellan

Born: 1480 Died: 1521
Duration of exploration: 1519–1522

Ferdinand Magellan grew up in Portugal and studied navigation and map-making. Inspired by Portuguese explorer Vasco da Gama, Magellan was desperate to go to sea. He joined various expeditions and began to plan his own. In the end, Magellan would meet a gruesome fate but his voyage would go down in history.

· 1 ·

Magellan planned to reach the Moluccas, known as the "Spice Islands," and bring back valuable spices. Like Christopher Columbus, he wanted to sail west from Europe to Asia, instead of east—the more common and safer route. The King of Spain financed the voyage and in September 1519, Magellan set out from Seville in Spain with a fleet of five ships.

· 5 ·

The grueling journey took 38 days. One ship was wrecked in the passage. In November, the three remaining ships finally reached a vast ocean. Magellan named it *Mar Pacifico* (Pacific Ocean) because the waters were so calm and the word "pacific" means peaceful. The fleet was now sailing into the largest ocean on Earth.

PACIFIC OCEAN

· 4 ·

Next, Magellan led the fleet down the coast of South America, searching for a way through the continent that would allow them to reach the ocean on the other side. At last, in October 1520, the fleet reached a passage of water at the bottom of South America (known today as the Magellan Strait) and began to sail through it.

· 2 ·

The first challenge was crossing the Atlantic Ocean. It took nearly two months, but at last Magellan reached Brazil on December 13. The fleet continued on to Argentina, where they stayed for four months. During this time Magellan spotted a peculiar type of flightless bird. It was a penguin! The species he discovered is known today as the Magellanic penguin.

· 3 ·

Over time, some of Magellan's captains became uneasy. There was a long way to go and the voyage had been tough so far. They planned to desert the expedition. Magellan found out and crushed the rebellion. He had two of his captains killed and left a third marooned on the Argentinian coast. All three were replaced by other members of the crew and the journey continued.

· 6 ·

Magellan's troubles were not over. Instead of the three days he had calculated to cross the Pacific Ocean, it took three and a half months. The food had almost run out and the men were forced to eat worm-riddled biscuits, and rats. Finally, the ships reached the Mariana Islands and from there, they continued to the Philippines where tragedy was waiting for them.

· 7 ·

Magellan got involved in a war between two chiefs, but his luck was over. He was wounded by a bamboo spear and died on April 27, 1521. So many of his crew were also killed that there were not enough men to sail three ships and one was abandoned. But the survivors decided to continue the voyage.

· 8 ·

After stopping in Brunei, the last two ships (the *Trinidad* and the *Vittoria*) finally reached the Moluccas on November 6, 1521. They loaded up with spices and set sail for home. But the *Trinidad* sprang a leak and was left behind, leaving the *Vittoria* to make the voyage back to Spain alone.

· 9 ·

Juan Sebastian Elcano was the last captain alive. With a small crew, he sailed across the Indian Ocean, around the Cape of Good Hope in South Africa, and up through the Atlantic Ocean, reaching Spain in September 1522. Three years had passed, Magellan was dead, and only 18 of the original 237 men had survived!

MAGELLAN'S EXPEDITION

NORTH AMERICA

EUROPE

ASIA

SPAIN
START / END

ATLANTIC OCEAN

AFRICA

PACIFIC OCEAN

MARIANA ISLANDS

BRUNEI

MOLUCCAS ISLANDS

SOUTH AMERICA

BRAZIL

INDIAN OCEAN

AUSTRALIA AND OCEANIA

ARGENTINA

Cape of Good Hope

MAGELLAN'S LEGACY

Despite the loss of so many lives the voyage was seen as a success. The spices that were brought back were more valuable than gold! But the biggest legacy of the journey is that it was the first voyage to go all the way around the Earth.

Hernán Cortés

Born: 1485 Died: 1547
Duration of exploration: 1518–1521

Hernán Cortés was born in Spain and left home in 1504 to sail to the New World of the Americas. He was 19 years old and in search of fame and fortune. Courageous, ruthless, and cunning, Cortés quickly rose to power in these newly conquered territories. In 1519, he led an expedition to modern-day Mexico that would cause the downfall of the Aztec Empire.

· 1 ·

In late 1518, Cortés was on the island of Cuba, a Spanish colony in the Caribbean Sea. The Cuban governor, Diego Velázquez, put Cortés in charge of an expedition to conquer Mexico. But the two men became fierce rivals and before Cortés left for Mexico, Velázquez cancelled the mission. Cortés ignored him and set sail in February 1519.

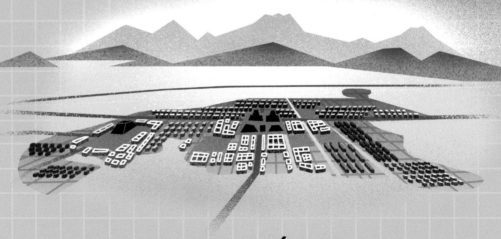

· 2 ·

The expedition included 11 ships and more than 500 soldiers. After stopping to take on board more soldiers and horses, Cortés landed on the coast of Veracruz in Mexico in March 1519. His first action was to claim the land for Spain. He then destroyed his own ships to stop any of his men from returning to Cuba!

· 4 ·

By November, Cortés had reached Tenochtitlan and was amazed by the city's size and grandeur. Tenochtitlan was founded in 1325 and built on an island in the middle of a lake, called Lake Texcoco.

· 3 ·

Most of central Mexico was governed by the Aztecs at the time. The Aztecs had been in power for over 170 years but were unpopular with many of the people they ruled. Cortés had heard of the wealth of the Aztecs and wanted to steal it. He convinced unhappy local people to join his troops and, in August 1519, he marched on Tenochtitlan, the capital of the Aztec Empire, at the head of a huge army.

· 5 ·

The Aztec emperor, Moctezuma, was wary of Cortés's huge army, so he welcomed him in peace and showered him with gifts. But when Cortés learned that several Spaniards stationed on the coast had been killed by Aztecs, he took Moctezuma hostage in his own palace and demanded a huge ransom.

· 6 ·

Back in Cuba, Velázquez had not forgotten that Cortés had defied him. In April 1520, he sent an army to Mexico. Cortés and his men managed to defeat Velázquez's troops and returned to Tenochtitlan. But Cortés found the city in uproar. Moctezuma had been killed. Cortés knew that his life was in danger and he fled.

· 7 ·

The Spaniards left Tenochtitlan in such a panic that much of the treasure they had stolen from the Aztecs was left behind. A year later, Cortés returned, determined to take revenge. For three months, his troops attacked the city, cutting off supplies and forcing the Aztecs to surrender. The siege ended with a Spanish victory and the fall of the Aztec Empire.

· 8 ·

Cortés claimed Tenochtitlan and its treasures for Spain and renamed it Mexico City. He set about destroying the ancient city, rebuilding it in the style of a European city. The Spanish king, Charles I, appointed Cortés governor of the land he had conquered. The king also honored Cortés with a coat of arms.

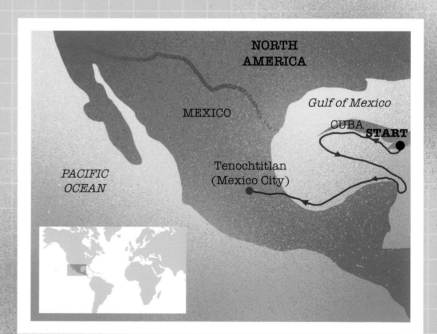

· 9 ·

Cortés didn't stop there. He was power-hungry and continued to invade more territories without permission. In 1528, he was ordered back to Spain. The king stripped Cortés of his title of governor in an attempt to control him. Cortés returned to Mexico with less authority but continued searching for new land.

· 10 ·

Cortés returned to Spain in 1541, a bitter man with huge debts. He had continued to ignore orders and was deeply unpopular with the king. Finally, he decided to return to Mexico, but fell seriously ill before he could leave. He died in Spain in December 1547 at the age of 62.

James Cook

Born: 1728 Died: 1779
Duration of exploration: 1768–1779

The English sailor, James Cook, learned to sail at the age of 17. He joined the Royal Navy and later went on to command three epic voyages, beginning in 1768. Although he was exploring in the name of science, Cook was also given secret missions! The missions would lead him to sail twice around the world and bring back fascinating information. But they would also cost him his life.

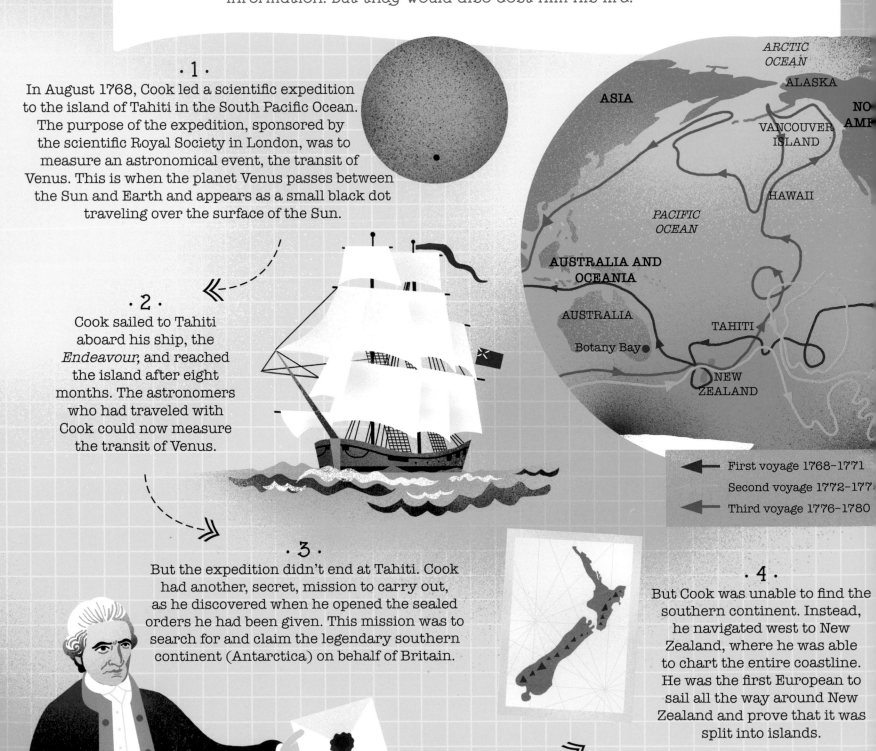

· 1 ·

In August 1768, Cook led a scientific expedition to the island of Tahiti in the South Pacific Ocean. The purpose of the expedition, sponsored by the scientific Royal Society in London, was to measure an astronomical event, the transit of Venus. This is when the planet Venus passes between the Sun and Earth and appears as a small black dot traveling over the surface of the Sun.

· 2 ·

Cook sailed to Tahiti aboard his ship, the *Endeavour*, and reached the island after eight months. The astronomers who had traveled with Cook could now measure the transit of Venus.

ARCTIC OCEAN

ALASKA

ASIA

NO
AM

VANCOUVER
ISLAND

HAWAII

PACIFIC
OCEAN

AUSTRALIA AND
OCEANIA

AUSTRALIA

TAHITI

Botany Bay

NEW
ZEALAND

⬅ First voyage 1768-1771
⬅ Second voyage 1772-177
⬅ Third voyage 1776-1780

· 3 ·

But the expedition didn't end at Tahiti. Cook had another, secret, mission to carry out, as he discovered when he opened the sealed orders he had been given. This mission was to search for and claim the legendary southern continent (Antarctica) on behalf of Britain.

· 4 ·

But Cook was unable to find the southern continent. Instead, he navigated west to New Zealand, where he was able to chart the entire coastline. He was the first European to sail all the way around New Zealand and prove that it was split into islands.

· 5 ·

Cook then set out for Australia. In April 1770, he moored the *Endeavour* in an inlet on the east coast. The crew were the first Europeans to land here. Cook named the inlet "Stingray Harbour" after the stingrays they saw in the water, but later changed the name to "Botany Bay" after the many plants. When the ship's botanist Joseph Banks saw a kangaroo, he wrote that it was "...as large as a greyhound, of a mouse color and very swift."

· 6 ·

Cook returned home, but in 1772 he began another voyage to search for the southern continent again. Cook's new ship *Resolution* traveled farther south than any had before, but despite months of sailing the crew failed to find new land. Eventually they were forced back by thick sea ice.

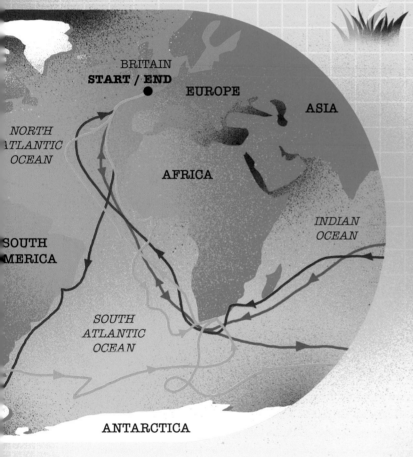

BRITAIN
START / END
EUROPE
ASIA
NORTH ATLANTIC OCEAN
AFRICA
INDIAN OCEAN
SOUTH AMERICA
SOUTH ATLANTIC OCEAN
ANTARCTICA

· 7 ·

In 1776, Cook set sail again. His secret instructions this time were to head to the Arctic to find the Northwest Passage (a sea route around the top of North America, joining the Pacific and Atlantic oceans). On the voyage north, Cook and his crew became the first Europeans to visit Hawaii. From here, they sailed up the Pacific coast of North America, reaching Vancouver Island in March 1778. Cook then sailed north, mapping the previously uncharted coastline as far as the Bering Strait, Alaska. But the expedition failed to find the Northwest Passage.

Captain Cook's Legacy

Cook's three voyages brought back a rich variety of information, from new maps, to exotic plants and accounts of unusual wildlife. Today, some believe that Cook began a new type of exploration, for peaceful, scientific purposes. Others argue that Cook's expeditions still colonized inhabited lands and had little care for local peoples.

· 8 ·

On the journey home in 1779, Cook returned to Hawaii. He and the crew were welcomed back but misunderstandings soon arose. Cook tried to solve matters by taking the local king hostage, but his plan went disastrously wrong. Cook and four of his men were killed. The surviving crew fled and arrived back in England a year later.

Lewis and Clark

Lewis Born: 1774 Died: 1809 / Clark Born: 1770 Died: 1838
Duration of exploration: 1804–1806

In 1803, President Thomas Jefferson chose two men to lead an expedition across America. The two leaders were Meriwether Lewis and William Clark. Their mission was to find a river route west from Missouri to the Pacific Ocean and open up the region for trade and settlement.

· 1 ·

In May 1804, Lewis and Clark set out from St. Louis, Missouri, with 43 men, a Newfoundland dog, and three boats loaded with food, weapons, medicine, and other supplies.

· 2 ·

They followed the Missouri River westward, passing plains where huge herds of buffalo roamed. They managed to cover an average distance of 15 miles a day along the muddy river, but often needed to push or even carry their boats.

· 3 ·

In November, they reached the lands of the Mandan Indians, a tribe of Native Americans. Lewis and Clark paused their journey to build a fort of log cabins where they could spend the long, cold winter.

· 4 ·

Lewis and Clark spent the winter learning survival skills from the local tribes and planning the next stage of their expedition. In early April 1805, they resumed the expedition. A Native American woman from the Lemhi Shoshone tribe, named Sacagawea, accompanied them as translator and guide, taking her two-month-old baby with her.

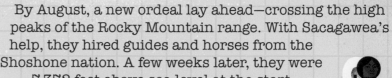

· 6 ·

By August, a new ordeal lay ahead—crossing the high peaks of the Rocky Mountain range. With Sacagawea's help, they hired guides and horses from the Shoshone nation. A few weeks later, they were 7,372 feet above sea level at the start of the Lemhi Pass, a trail through the snow-capped Bitterroot mountains. The weather was bitterly cold and food ran short, but Sacagawea led them safely across.

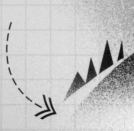

· 5 ·

It was a dangerous journey through unknown territory. One day, while exploring along the riverside, Lewis was chased by a grizzly bear. In June 1805, they reached five steep waterfalls called the Great Falls of the Missouri River. The only way past was to haul the boats overland around them.

· 7 ·

In early October, Lewis and Clark traded in their horses and built five dugout canoes. The fast waters of the Clearwater River carried them to the Columbia River, the largest in the Northwest. At last, on November 7, Lewis and Clark caught sight of the Pacific Ocean for the first time. Two weeks later, they finally reached the coast.

· 9 ·

Lewis and Clark never found a river-only route all the way to the Pacific. But their expedition was still a triumph. They had never given up! They made useful maps and brought back details of many new species of plants and animals. Today, they're remembered as American heroes.

· 8 ·

The men built another fort, Fort Clatsop, and settled in for the winter. In late March 1806, Lewis and Clark set out on the long journey home. In September of that year, nearly two and a half years after they had left St. Louis, Lewis and Clark reached home. They had traveled more than 7,500 miles over rivers, plains, and mountains!

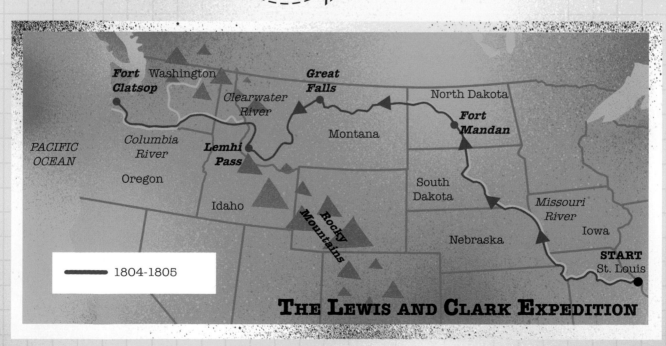

THE LEWIS AND CLARK EXPEDITION

29

David Livingstone

Born: 1813 Died: 1873
Duration of exploration: 1866–1873

The Scottish explorer, David Livingstone, worked as a medical missionary, introducing Christianity to people in Africa. For more than 20 years, he explored vast areas of the huge continent. These expeditions made him famous, but today he is best known for his extraordinary last journey.

· 1 ·

In January 1866, the Royal Geographical Society in London sent Livingstone to look for the source of the Nile River in Africa. Livingstone had already had many adventures—even fighting off a lion on a previous expedition but this last journey was to be the most difficult, lasting five years and eventually costing him his life.

· 2 ·

Livingstone began his expedition on Zanzibar, a small island off the coast of modern-day Tanzania in East Africa. He gathered a team of local people to assist him on the hazardous journey. Livingstone believed that slavery was wrong and freed slaves were part of his group.

· 3 ·

The expedition sailed south from Zanzibar to the Ruvuma River. Livingstone's plan was to travel along the river to Lake Nyasa, then north overland to Lake Tanganyika to explore the surrounding area for the source of the Nile. Other explorers of the time believed the source was farther north, either at Lake Albert or at Lake Victoria.

· 5 ·

Livingstone was determined to carry on. He set out toward Lake Tanganyika with a small team. Their route lay partly through treacherous swamplands. A very long, difficult journey was ahead.

· 4 ·

Disaster struck the expedition almost immediately. In early August 1866, Livingstone reached Lake Nyasa, but many of his team had deserted him on the way, taking his precious supplies and medicines with them.

· 6 ·

Livingstone's health was failing. He arranged for medicines to be sent to Ujiji, a town near Lake Tanganyika, and he reluctantly traveled there with slave traders, needing the safety they could provide. The journey took more than two years! On the way, Livingstone traveled farther west than any European before, passing Lake Mweru, Lake Bangweulu, and the Lualaba River.

· 7 ·

At last, in March 1869, Livingstone reached Ujiji. By now he was suffering from pneumonia and cholera. The situation worsened when he found that the supplies and medicines he was expecting had been stolen. Livingstone had to stop his expedition and seek help from the slave traders again. They took him to Bambára in Mozambique, where he was trapped for months by the rainy season.

Map

DEMOCRATIC REPUBLIC OF THE CONGO

Lake Victoria

Lualaba River

Lake Tanganyika

Ujiji

TANZANIA

INDIAN OCEAN

ZANZIBAR

Lake Mweru

Lake Nyasa

Ruvuma River

Lake Bangweulu

MALAWI

ZAMBIA

MOZAMBIQUE

ZIMBABWE

Bambára

● Countries Livingstone visited

● Places Livingstone visited

· 8 ·

Eventually, Livingstone was able to travel and continue his mission. He was exploring the banks of the Lualaba River when he witnessed the massacre of hundreds of Africans by slave traders in the region. Livingstone was horrified and his distress led to illness. He was forced to make the 250-mile trek back to Ujiji. Seriously ill, he was carried most of the way.

· 9 ·

Back home in Britain, people feared that Livingstone was dead. They hadn't heard from him in years! Henry Morton Stanley, an American journalist, set out to find him. Two years later, in 1871, he found Livingstone, gravely unwell, in Ujiji.

· 10 ·

Stanley tried to persuade Livingstone to return home, but he refused. He wanted to continue his mission to find the source of the Nile. Sadly, it wasn't meant to be. In 1873, Livingstone died, never knowing that the source was, in fact, Lake Victoria. His body was taken back to Britain, but his heart was buried in Africa beside a Mupundu tree.

Mary Kingsley

Born: 1862 Died: 1900
Duration of exploration: 1893–1900

Mary Kingsley's father was an English doctor, who traveled widely for his work. Mary loved hearing his stories and longed to go exploring, too. In 1892, after both of her parents had died, Mary was left some money and time to herself. She made the courageous decision to follow her dreams.

· 1 ·

In August 1893, Mary set sail for Africa. At the time, exploration was considered unsuitable for women—it was dangerous and people thought women couldn't do it. But Mary had grown up reading her father's books and dreamed of visiting far-off places, so she persisted. She said that she was collecting material for a book her father had been writing and set off on her adventure.

· 2 ·

Mary arrived in Sierra Leone, then traveled to Luanda, Angola, where she voyaged along the River Congo on a steamer boat. She spent four months in Africa, traveling to modern-day Guinea and Nigeria, exploring mangrove swamps and living with the local Fjort people. She learned many skills for surviving in the African jungles. In December 1893 she headed back to England, but her adventures were far from over.

· 4 ·

While exploring the forest, Mary had a near fatal accident. She fell into a hidden pit, lined with long, wooden spikes, used to trap elephants. Her life was saved by chance as the Victorian dress she always wore cushioned her landing.

· 3 ·

Her first trip was a success and she had collected specimens of rare river fish and reptiles that she presented to the British Museum. The museum decided to fund her next voyage and a year later, Mary was back in Africa. This time she went to Gabon and traveled by canoe down the Ogooué River, deep into the dense rain forest.

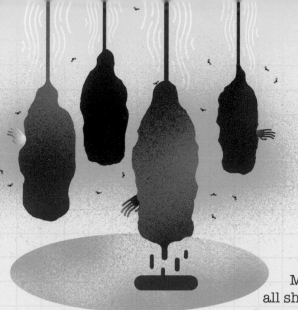

· 5 ·

Mary wanted to learn all she could about African religions and rituals. She did this by befriending local communities and using her nursing skills to gain their trust. She spent time in the village of Efoua, home of the Fang tribe of cannibals. With gruesome bags of human hands and heads hanging from the huts, most people would have been afraid, but Mary stayed and learned all she could about them.

· 6 ·

During her travels in Africa, Mary faced many dangers, including disease, storms, leopards, and crocodiles! She also encountered physical challenges and was the first European woman to climb to the top of Mount Cameroon, one of Africa's highest mountains.

· 8 ·

In 1900, Mary made one last journey, this time to modern-day South Africa, where she volunteered as a nurse, caring for soldiers in the Boer War. Sadly, she died of typhoid on June 3, 1900 and was buried at sea as she had always wanted.

· 7 ·

When Mary returned home in 1895, she was greeted like a celebrity—she even had three new species of fish named after her! She gave lectures about her travels, and wrote two best-selling books on her adventures. In these books she described the people and sights she had seen and criticized the religious and colonial missions that Europeans were leading.

- ● Countries Kingsley visited
- ● Places Kingsley visited

NIGERIA

CAMEROON

EQUATORIAL GUINEA

Ogooué River

THE REPUBLIC OF CONGO

GABON

Congo River

DEMOCRATIC REPUBLIC OF THE CONGO

Luanda

ANGOLA

Kingsley's adventures were mainly in West Africa.

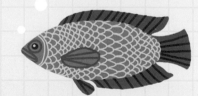

KINGSLEY'S LEGACY

Mary Kingsley was a pioneer. She documented rare animal species, climbed mountains, and proved that women could explore the world and create change. Many Europeans thought that African culture was not important. Mary challenged their ideas and helped change these attitudes.

Robert Peary

Born: 1856 Died: 1920
Duration of exploration: 1908–1909

Robert Peary made several expeditions to the Arctic in the late 19th and early 20th centuries. He explored and mapped Greenland and learned survival skills from the Inuit people. His dream was to be the first person to reach the North Pole. Whether or not he succeeded is still debated today!

· 1 ·

Robert Peary had the idea of being the first man to reach the North Pole in the 1880s when he served in the US Navy. In 1866, with $500 from his mother, Peary made his first expedition to the Arctic. He planned to cross Greenland by dog sled but had to turn back after 100 miles due to lack of food. But this was just the beginning of Peary's adventures in the Arctic!

· 2 ·

In 1891, Peary returned to Greenland. This time he was accompanied by a team, including his wife Josephine and assistant Matthew Henson, an African-American he had met in 1887. Henson would go on to accompany Peary on all of his subsequent adventures and become a great explorer himself. On this expedition, Peary wanted to determine whether or not Greenland was an island—people suspected it was, but there had never been any proof.

· 3 ·

Again, things did not go to plan. While sailing through dangerous sea ice, the tiller (steering device) spun out of control and hit Peary, breaking two bones in his leg. He spent six months recuperating with Josephine by his side, at a camp they built and named Red Cliff. During this time Peary studied Inuit survival skills, such as building igloos and wearing heavy fur skins to keep warm. In May 1892, with his leg healed, Peary and his team finally set out across the ice. By August he was back at the camp with the news that Greenland was indeed an island!

· 4 ·

After several more expeditions, Peary set off on his final Arctic adventure in 1908. This time he had 23 men and a new ship, the *Roosevelt*, and his mission was the one which he had dreamed of for years—to reach the North Pole!

· 5 ·

On February 28, 1909, Peary led his men and husky dogs from their base on Ellesmere Island over the frozen ocean. The men took turns skiing ahead to warn of hazards, such as crevasses (deep cracks in the ice). Some men were given the task of carrying essential equipment and laying stores along the way for the return party. Once the support team had left the stores and turned back as planned, only Peary, Henson, and four Inuit dog-handlers remained to make the final dash to the Pole.

· 6 ·

After marching in perfect conditions, Peary believed he had reached the North Pole on April 6, 1909. He took a photo of the men, with Henson holding the American flag, and headed home to tell the world of their success. However, many people said that Peary could not have made it to the Pole and back to base in just 16 days.

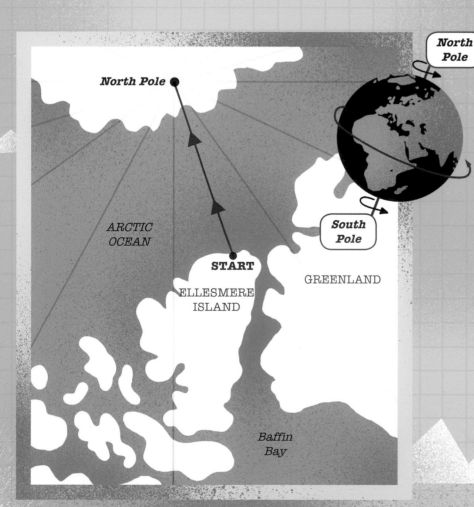

· 7 ·

This was not the only setback. Rival American explorer, Frederick Cook, also claimed to have reached the North Pole, in 1908, beating Peary by a year! Eventually a court ruled that Cook had not reached the North Pole. But many doubted whether Peary had made it, either. In 2005, British explorer Tom Avery recreated Peary's final march to the Pole, using replica sleds and equipment. In the end, Avery was convinced that Peary was indeed the first man to reach the North Pole, but still not everyone agrees, and the truth seems unlikely to ever be discovered.

Roald Amundsen

Born: 1872 Died: 1928
Duration of exploration: 1910–1912

Growing up in Norway, Roald Amundsen dreamed of being a polar explorer. But to please his parents, he trained as a doctor, while secretly reading the books of famous explorers and getting physically fit. His mother died when he was 21 and shortly afterward Amundsen gave up medicine for a life of adventure. He would go on to achieve things no other person had before.

· 1 ·

In 1897, Amundsen joined an expedition to Antarctica. This was his first real taste of life as an explorer. The trip did not go smoothly, with the ship becoming frozen into the sea ice for months and the crew at risk of starvation and scurvy. But they made it home alive and Amundsen used his experiences to help him on future expeditions.

TELEGRAM

DATE: _September 8, 1910_

TO: _Captain Robert F Scott, SS Tina Nora, Melbourne_

MESSAGE: _Beg to inform you Fram proceeding Antarctica_

· 4 ·

Amundsen set sail from Norway in June 1910, but he kept his plans secret until September, when he sent Scott a telegram. In January 1911, after six months of sailing, his crew reached the Bay of Whales in the Ross Sea, and set up camp. The men spent the winter meticulously planning and laying stores on their route to the South Pole.

· 2 ·

Between 1903 and 1906, Amundsen led another expedition, through the Northwest Passage between the Atlantic and Pacific oceans. During this time, he learned valuable Arctic survival skills from local Inuit people, such as how to use sled dogs and wear animal skins.

· 3 ·

In 1909, Amundsen planned his next expedition. The North Pole had already been reached by Robert Peary. But no one had made it to the South Pole yet, although British explorer, Robert Scott, was planning an expedition. Amundsen decided he would race Scott there in his ship, *Fram*, which was specially built to cope with polar ice.

· 5 ·

On October 19, Amundsen set out across the Ross Ice Shelf with four men and four sleds, each pulled by 13 dogs. They made good progress and by mid-November they had crossed the Transantarctic Mountains, the halfway point of their journey.

· 6 ·

Next, they climbed the Axel Heiberg Glacier, riddled with crevasses and blocks of ice, to reach the Polar Plateau, a vast, flat expanse of ice around the South Pole. Here they made camp and prepared to make their final push for the Pole, but a blizzard forced them to stay in camp for another four grueling days.

· 7 ·

Finally, on December 14, 1911, Amundsen and his men became the first people to reach the South Pole (33 days before Scott). After planting the Norwegian flag and leaving a small tent and a note for Scott, they returned safely to base. Though Scott eventually made it to the Pole, he and his team never made it back. Amundsen would go on to say that it was his careful planning that had led to success.

Norge, the airship that flew Amundsen to the North Pole.

AMUNDSEN'S LEGACY

After the South Pole, Amundsen continued exploring. He attempted various expeditions exploring the Arctic Ocean but was mostly unsuccessful. In 1926, he made history again by being part of the first crew to reach the North Pole by airship. But on June 18, 1928, Amundsen disappeared with five others while flying in a rescue mission in the Arctic. The plane was thought to have crashed in heavy fog, but the wreck and the bodies of Amundsen and the crew were never recovered.

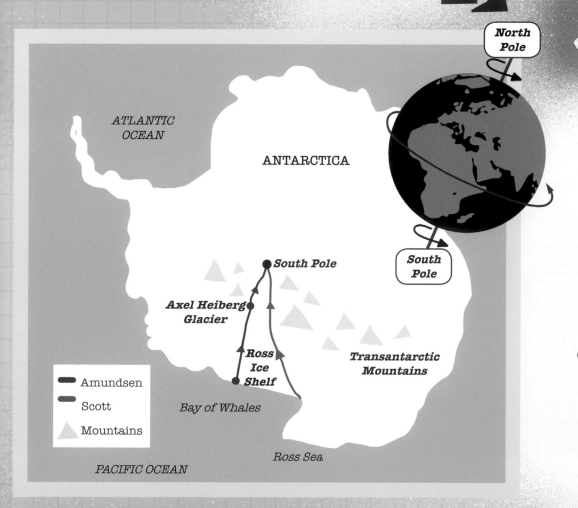

ATLANTIC OCEAN

ANTARCTICA

North Pole

South Pole

South Pole

Axel Heiberg Glacier

Ross Ice Shelf

Transantarctic Mountains

Bay of Whales

Ross Sea

PACIFIC OCEAN

- Amundsen
- Scott
- Mountains

Ernest Shackleton

Born: 1874 Died: 1922
Duration of exploration: 1914–1916

Ernest Shackleton was a polar explorer from Britain. In 1907, he came within 100 miles of the South Pole before illness forced him back. Seven years later, Shackleton planned a daring journey, never accomplished before—the 1,800-mile crossing of Antarctica from west to east.

MEN WANTED

FOR HAZARDOUS JOURNEY. LOW WAGES, BITTER COLD, LONG HOURS OF COMPLETE DARKNESS. SAFE RETURN DOUBTFUL. HONOR AND RECOGNITION IN EVENT OF SUCCESS.

· 1 ·

Legend says that Shackleton placed a newspaper ad for his crew, and more than 5,000 people applied! Shackleton selected scientists, surgeons, and sailors. The crew also included 69 dogs, brought to pull sleds on the trip, and Mrs. Chippy, the ship's cat.

· 2 ·

The expedition left England, on August 8, 1914, on the ship *Endurance*. In early November, they reached South Georgia, an island close to South America, where the crew spent a month preparing. On December 5, Shackleton sailed for Antarctica.

· 3 ·

Finding a passage through the icy water to Antarctica was very slow. In January, they picked up speed, but thick ice soon closed around the ship. By January 19, 1915, the *Endurance* and its men were trapped!

· 4 ·

Shackleton realized they would be stuck until September (springtime in Antarctica), when the ice would hopefully thaw. The crew faced months of waiting. The dogs were taken off the ship and put in kennels made of ice and snow, called dogloos.

· 7 ·

By April 1916, their supplies were low. Then the ice began to break up! Shackleton ordered the crew into the lifeboats and they rowed as hard as they could in search of land. The crew spent the next five days cramped together, exhausted and terrified.

· 8 ·

At last, they reached Elephant Island, an uninhabited place rarely visited by ships. With a sick crew and slim chance of rescue, Shackleton made a plan. On April 24, he and five men rowed out in search of South Georgia. Fifteen harrowing days of storms, huge waves, hurricane winds, and near capsizes followed.

· 6 ·

Finally, September arrived, but as the ice melted, the ship splintered under the pressure! Shackleton gave the order to abandon ship. The crew camped on floating ice, hoping to drift to land. The expedition was over—now, Shackleton's only goal was to keep his crew alive.

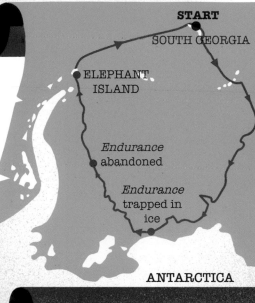

START
SOUTH GEORGIA
ELEPHANT ISLAND
Endurance abandoned
Endurance trapped in ice
ANTARCTICA

· 9 ·

They landed on South Georgia on May 9, but far away from any people. Shackleton, with two of his men, crossed the island on foot, over mountains that had never been climbed before. The journey was agonizing, but they did it in 36 hours. They found some local workers and urgently planned the rescue of the crew left behind.

· 10 ·

Finally, on August 30, Shackleton returned to Elephant Island to rescue his stranded men. All of the crew lived—it was a remarkable feat of survival! Following the expedition, most of the crew were awarded medals for their bravery. It took 40 years before another group of explorers crossed Antarctica.

· 5 ·

Over the months, the ship slowly drifted north with the ice. The crew took part in activities to lift their spirits—they even played soccer on the ice!

Amelia Earhart

Born: 1897 Disappeared: 1937
Duration of exploration: March–July 1937

Amelia Earhart got hooked on flying as a young woman. In 1932, she became the first female pilot to fly solo across the Atlantic Ocean. Following this, Earhart planned a fearless adventure—a flight around the world at the Equator, which had never been attempted before.

· 1 ·

On March 17, 1937, Earhart set off with navigator Fred Noonan. The first leg of the journey was from California to Hawaii. Earhart was flying a Lockheed Electra, which had the latest radio and navigational equipment.

· 2 ·

The journey was swift and the plane set a speed record as it reached Hawaii. On March 20, they began the next leg. But the Electra crashed on takeoff! Witnesses saw a tire burst and the plane skid along the runway. Earhart and Noonan were unharmed, but the Electra had to be shipped back to California and took weeks to be repaired.

NORTH
AMERICA

START
California

HAWAII

ATLANT.
OCEAN

Equator

SOUTH
AMERICA

PACIFIC
OCEAN

· 3 ·

Undeterred, on May 21, Earhart and Noonan set off again (heading east this time). By June 15th, they had crossed the Atlantic Ocean, traveled through three continents, and made a total of 18 stops in order to rest and refuel. Earhart was so popular and her flight around the world so famous, that crowds would gather where she and Noonan landed.

· 4 ·

On June 17, Earhart and Noonan left modern-day Pakistan for India. Facing strong winds and heavy rain, they flew on to Java, where they saw some amazing sights, including active volcanoes. The next stop was Australia, on the way to New Guinea. After that there would be just two stops left on their flight—Howland Island and Honolulu, Hawaii.

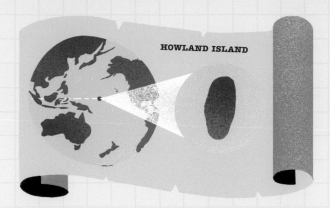

HOWLAND ISLAND

· 5 ·

On July 2, 1937, Earhart and Noonan took off from New Guinea. Only 6,835 miles lay ahead, but the most dangerous part of the journey had just begun. The next stop was Howland Island, a tiny, uninhabited landmass in the Pacific Ocean just two miles long and half a mile wide. It would be difficult for Earhart and Noonan to see the island from so high up, but it was the only place where they could refuel.

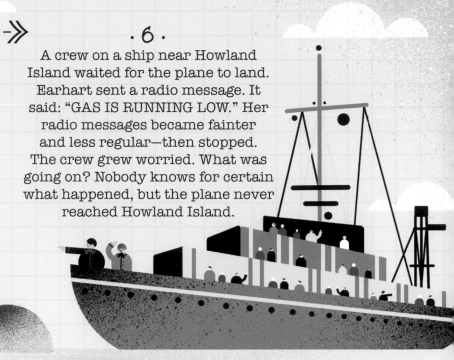

· 6 ·

A crew on a ship near Howland Island waited for the plane to land. Earhart sent a radio message. It said: "GAS IS RUNNING LOW." Her radio messages became fainter and less regular—then stopped. The crew grew worried. What was going on? Nobody knows for certain what happened, but the plane never reached Howland Island.

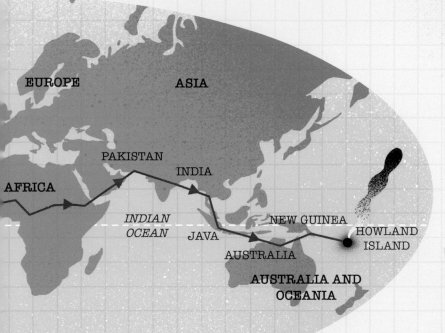

EUROPE   ASIA

AFRICA

PAKISTAN

INDIA

INDIAN OCEAN   NEW GUINEA

JAVA

AUSTRALIA   HOWLAND ISLAND

AUSTRALIA AND OCEANIA

ARCTICA

· 7 ·

An enormous rescue effort featuring 66 aircraft and nine ships was launched by the US Navy to find the missing pilot and her navigator. But Earhart, Noonan, and the Electra were never seen again.

MISSING AT SEA

EARHART'S PLANE LOST AT SEA

· 8 ·

There have been many theories about what happened—including that Earhart was a spy! It's likely that the plane ran out of fuel and crashed into the water. Some people, however, believe that Earhart and Noonan were stranded and eventually died on a remote island. No trace of the Electra or proven remains of the explorers have ever been found, even using modern deep-sea technology. The mystery remains unsolved!

Norgay and Hillary

Norgay Born: 1914 Died: 1986 / Hillary Born: 1919 Died: 2008
Duration of exploration: April 12–May 29, 1953

Mount Everest in the Himalayas is the world's highest mountain. In the early 20th century many people tried to reach the top, but the climb was risky and some died in the attempt. Then, on May 29, 1953, Tenzing Norgay from Nepal and Edmund Hillary from New Zealand made history when, as part of the British Everest Expedition, they stood on top of the world.

· 1 ·

Norgay and Tenzing were part of the British Everest Expedition. The team was made up of 15 mountaineers, 22 Sherpas (local guides), and over 300 porters. The plan was to send groups up the mountain in stages to find routes and establish camps. There were many possible dangers, including frostbite and avalanches. But the men were not put off and Base Camp (where equipment and supplies were stored) was set up on April 12.

· 2 ·

Six weeks later, eight camps had successfully been made on the way up the mountain. On May 28, Norgay and Hillary set up Camp 9, 1,600 feet from the summit. They pitched their tent and snatched a few hours' sleep. Waking at 4 a.m., they prepared for the climb to the top. It was so cold that Hillary had to "cook" his frozen boots over the camp stove to thaw them!

· 3 ·

At 6:30 a.m., after breakfast, Norgay and Hillary started for the South Summit, a smaller peak below the main summit. The two climbers wore triple-layered clothing and tinted eye masks to prevent snow blindness. They carried canned fish, soup, canned apricots, and tea, and they ate regularly.

· 4 ·

It was a hard climb through deep snow covered by an icy crust. Air has less oxygen at high altitudes so as well as heavy backpacks, the men carried oxygen tanks to help their breathing. By 9 a.m. Norgay and Hillary had reached the South Summit. The only route to the main summit was up a treacherous, narrow ridge. Roped together for safety, in case one of them slipped, the climbers went on.

· 5 ·

A bigger hazard now loomed ahead—a near-vertical rock face lay across the ridge, blocking their path. The massive cliff was about 40 feet high. Unless Hillary and Norgay could figure out a way to climb it, their hopes of reaching the summit were dashed.

· 6 ·

Hillary saw a crack between the rock and the huge overhang of ice next to it. He decided to use this narrow space as his route up the rock face. Squeezing inside, it took all his strength to force himself upward. Norgay slowly followed. It was the first time anyone had climbed this rock face, which was later named Hillary Step.

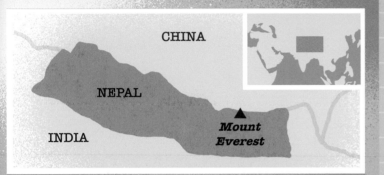

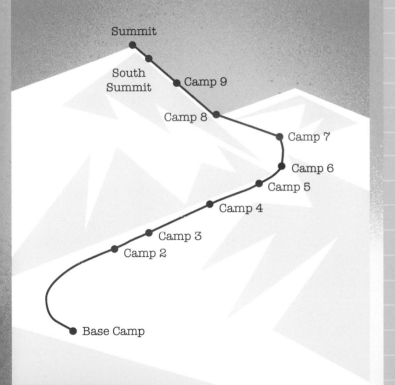

· 7 ·

By now, Norgay and Hillary had been climbing for more than 24 hours. Their oxygen supplies were low and the exhausted pair were finding it hard to figure out how far they were from the top. Finally, they noticed the way ahead starting to slope down and a small, snowy mound—the summit!

· 8 ·

At 11:30 a.m. on May 29, the two men stood on the summit of Mount Everest at the colossal height of 29,030 feet! After they had planted several flags, Hillary photographed Norgay clutching his ice axe with the United Kingdom's flag attached to it.

· 10 ·

The news spread around the world. Norgay and Hillary became stars and were given many honors and awards. For years, they continued to take part in expeditions. Fifty years after their fathers' climb, Norgay's son, Jamling, and Hillary's son, Peter, climbed Everest together.

EVEREST CONQUERED

· 9 ·

After only 15 minutes, Hillary and Norgay began their return journey, following the same path they had taken up. Just two hours later, at 2 p.m., they arrived back at Camp 9 and collapsed exhausted in their tent. A day or so later, Norgay and Hillary were back at Base Camp.

Neil Armstrong

Born: 1930 Died: 2012
Duration of exploration: July 16–24 1969

Neil Armstrong developed a love of flying at a young age. He took flying lessons while in high school in Ohio and flew his first solo flight at 16 years old—before he had even earned his driver's license on the ground. Armstrong's passion influenced his career and led him to become one of the most famous explorers on Earth—and beyond!

· 1 ·

Neil Armstrong began his career as a pilot in the US Navy, where he stayed until he was 21. Armstrong later worked as a test pilot for about 10 years, flying aircraft to test their performance. He had many close calls during this time, with engines failing and terrifying rough landings. But these experiences would help him prepare for the next chapter in his life.

· 3 ·

Armstrong and eight other astronauts were selected. He spent the following years training to prepare for the mission. The work was highly dangerous. Some men died and Armstrong nearly lost his life during one simulation when the controls of his aircraft began to fail—he ejected from his seat and opened his parachute just in time!

· 2 ·

In 1962, Armstrong successfully applied to become an astronaut for the National Aeronautics and Space Administration (NASA). At the time, Russia and the US were in a race to be the first to explore space. The Russians were in the lead in this "Space Race"— but the US weren't giving up. The next big step was to send humans to the Moon.

· 4 ·

Finally, at 9:32 a.m. on July 16, 1969, after seven years of training and planning, Armstrong and two colleagues, Buzz Aldrin and Michael Collins, blasted off from Cape Kennedy, Florida, on board the Apollo 11 spacecraft. Armstrong was the Commander, while Aldrin and Collins were pilots. Armstrong's wife and sons watched from a boat as he was launched up into the unknown.

· 5 ·

Inside the spacecraft, it was small and confined, but the astronauts were prepared for this. What they couldn't prepare for was the fear they would feel. Armstrong's heart rate peaked at 110 beats per minute as they took off! But the mission was going well. After three days, Apollo 11 went into orbit around the Moon as planned.

· 6 ·

On July 20, Armstrong and Aldrin crawled into *Eagle*, the lunar module spacecraft that Aldrin would pilot and land on the Moon. Meanwhile, Collins stayed in the command module, *Columbia*, to provide communication between the astronauts and the team on Earth. Once they were safely on the surface, Armstrong said, "The Eagle has landed."

The Eagle has landed.

· 7 ·

After a rest, the astronauts put on their life-support system backpacks. Each pack had a vital oxygen supply, temperature control, and two-way radio. Finally, they opened the hatch, and Armstrong climbed down the ladder and stepped onto the Moon. "That's one small step for a man, one giant leap for mankind," he famously said.

· 8 ·

On Earth, millions of people watched in amazement as Armstrong became the first human in history to walk on the Moon. NASA had been able to develop cameras advanced and robust enough to survive the rocket launch and journey through space, so that the whole world could watch.

· 9 ·

Back on the Moon, Aldrin and Armstrong took photos, collected samples of Moon rock and dust, and set up a series of scientific experiments. They also planted an American flag on the Moon's surface. They had to stiffen the flag with wire to make it look as if it were flying, because there is no air, or wind, on the Moon.

· 11 ·

The men were greeted as heroes, with parades, celebrations, and awards. Neil Armstrong would go down in history as one of the most remarkable explorers of all time and his famous words would be remembered by billions of people.

· 10 ·

The astronauts returned to the *Eagle* after only two and half hours. They set off and reunited with Collins in the command module and began their journey back to Earth. On July 24, *Columbia* splashed down in the Pacific Ocean as planned. The astronauts were alive and well.

Ellen MacArthur

Born: 1976
Duration of exploration: November 28, 2004–February 7, 2005

British-born Ellen MacArthur was interested in sailing from a young age. She even saved up her lunch money for years in order to buy her first boat. After gaining fame and recognition for a number of sailing achievements—including sailing single-handed around Britain—MacArthur set her sights on a new goal: breaking the record for sailing solo around the world.

· 1 ·

On November 28, 2004, MacArthur set sail from France on a journey of more than 26,000 miles. She knew she faced a difficult task. In her log, she wrote, "It's going to be a tough one ... I can feel it, and really know that I am going to have to dig very, very deep. The most important thing though ... is that I really want to enjoy this."

· 2 ·

Her boat, the *B&Q*, had been specially made for her. It had a tiny living area down below, with room for a bunk, sink, gas stove, and chart table. This would be MacArthur's home for the next three months.

· 4 ·

MacArthur now entered the Southern Ocean, famous for being rough and challenging to sail on. She spent weeks, including Christmas Day, in these waters, being thrown around by enormous waves, facing freezing temperatures, and battling storm-force winds. But she couldn't hunker down safely—she had to keep an eye out for danger and avoid crashing into icebergs the size of container ships!

· 3 ·

Being on the open sea alone and having to sail and maintain the boat was hard work. After six days, MacArthur's hands were covered in sores, but she didn't give up. She sailed past the western coasts of Spain, Portugal, and Africa, and through the doldrums (parts of the ocean around the Equator prone to sudden storms and unpredictable winds) before rounding the Cape of Good Hope, South Africa.

· 5 ·

Exhausted, MacArthur wrote in her log, "The last three days of sailing have been undoubtedly the worst of my career ... I have never been as tired as that in my life." Then, on January 12, MacArthur celebrated sailing around Cape Horn, at the southern tip of South America. She had left the Southern Ocean at last.

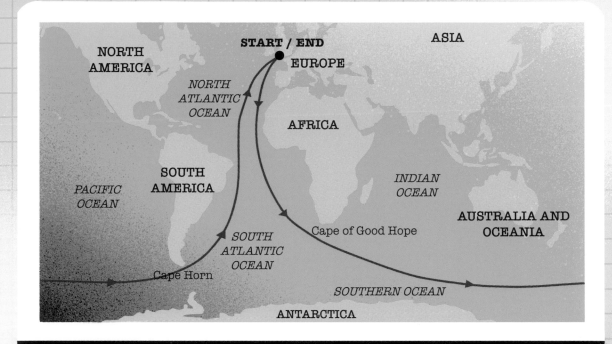

· 6 ·

Unfortunately, the South Atlantic Ocean proved to be just as treacherous. During one petrifying storm, MacArthur feared her boat would be broken to pieces. The waves were mountainous. The mainsail became damaged and MacArthur had to climb the 100-foot mast to patch it up. Though exhausted and bruised, she couldn't afford to stop, so she sailed on.

· 7 ·

MacArthur was now on the homeward leg of her epic voyage, sailing up the east coast of South America. On day 63, January 29, 2005, she had a very narrow miss. She spotted a whale, about 30 feet long, in front of the boat. She braced herself for a collision, but the whale dove beneath the water, just in time.

· 8 ·

MacArthur knew that if she continued at her pace and faced no problems, she could break the record. The pressure was building and her nerves made it hard for her to sleep. Finally, on February 7, 2005, MacArthur crossed the finish line. Her voyage had taken 71 days, 14 hours, 18 minutes and 33 seconds, breaking the previous record by over 32 hours!

DAME MacARTHUR

· 9 ·

MacArthur had survived some of the stormiest seas on the planet, alone, on freeze-dried food, and only five hours of sleep every 24 hours (divided into 15-minute naps). A day after her record win, she was greeted by huge cheering crowds as she sailed into Falmouth harbor, UK. She was given the title of "Dame" by Queen Elizabeth, making her one of the youngest people to have received this honor.

First published in the UK in 2019 by

Ivy Kids

An imprint of The Quarto Group

The Old Brewery

6 Blundell Street

London N7 9BH

United Kingdom

www.QuartoKnows.com

A CIP record for this book is available from the Library of Congress.

ISBN: 978-1-78240-747-8

This book was conceived, designed & produced by

Ivy Kids

58 West Street, Brighton BN1 2RA, United Kingdom

PUBLISHER Susan Kelly

CREATIVE DIRECTOR Michael Whitehead

MANAGING EDITOR Susie Behar

ART DIRECTOR Hanri van Wyk

DESIGNER Claire Munday

IN-HOUSE DESIGNER Kate Haynes

PROJECT EDITOR Hannah Dove

ASSISTANT EDITOR Lucy Menzies

Manufactured in Ljubljana, Slovenia DZ012019

1 3 5 7 9 10 8 6 4 2

MIX
Paper from
responsible sources
FSC® C110418